GERMAN TACTICAL DOCTRINE

GW01081203

PREPARED BY

MILITARY INTELLIGENCE SERVICE

War Department

December 20, 1942

German troops on the march in Greece.

FOREWORD

Frederick the Great, as the result of his experiences in the Seven Years' War, is credited with establishing the first General Staff in the history of military forces. This Staff was created to handle administrative details, thus releasing more time to the commanders for tactical considerations. It was not, however, until 1810 that Frederick's successors established a school to train officers for General Staff duty. Because successful military results were achieved, France, Great Britain, the United States, Japan, and other countries based the formation of their General Staffs upon the model set by Germany.

Beginning with Scharnhorst, such distinguished leaders and strategists as Moltke (the elder) and von Schlieffen were closely associated with the development of the General Staff School, which operated continuously from. 1810 until the outbreak of World War I. Subsequent to that war the Versailles Treaty forbade the continuance of the school, and it was not until 1933 that the Kriegsakademie, as the Germans call it, was officially reopened in the Berlin location that it was occupying at the outbreak of World War II.

During the years from 1935 to 1939, the United States was allowed to send four individual officers to take the course. From their illuminating reports it is possible to learn the trend of German methods and teachings up to Hitler's attack on Poland. Our observers unanimously agreed that the main-body of doctrine taught at the Kriegsakademie — the body of doc trine that underlies the German warfare of today — is set forth in Truppenführung, the German tactical bible so very similar in matter and precept to our own FM 100-5, Field Service Regulations, Operations.

The following partial resume of doctrine[1] taught at the Kriegsakademie is actually a practical adaptation of

---

[1] The Military Intelligence Service has published the following

relevant parts of Truppenführung. It will be noted that this resume (ignoring the factor of translation) is written almost exactly as a German would instruct Germans. This faithfulness to the tone of the original lectures has been made possible because of the extremely adequate reports which were made by the U. S. officer-students.

Throughout, striking similarities will be observed between German tactical doctrine and that set down in pertinent manuals of the U. S. Army. U. S. officers, however, should not be misled by the similarities to over-look the differences that also exist. With regard to one of the basic similarities in doctrine, it has been pointed out by one of our Kriegsakademie graduates that "Owing to the phlegmatic nature of the German individual, initiative and aggressive action have to be forced on the lower leaders and staff, rank and file, whereas we possess these characteristics as a natural heritage."

---

bulletins which describe various aspects of German military methods: "The German Armored Division," Information Bulletin, No. 18, June 15, 1942; "German Methods of Warfare in the Libyan Desert," Information Bulletin, No. 20, July 5, 1942; "The German Armored Army," Special Series, No. 4, October 17, 1942; "The Development of German Defensive Tactics in Cyrenaiea — 1941," Special Series, No, 5, October 19, 1942; "Artillery in the Desert," Special Series, No. 6, November 25, 1942. Information about specific organizations and weapons may be found in TM 30-450, Handbook on German Military Forces.

A German Commander at Stalingrad

Section I. POST OF THE COMMANDER

The personal influence of the commander upon his troops is of the greatest significance. He must be located where he can most effectively lead. On the march he should be as far forward as security permits, and his location should be definitely known by the members of his staff so that all reports may reach him promptly. In the attack his command post should be located as far forward as possible, yet protected from hostile fire so as to insure undisturbed operation; for tactical reasons, the post is placed near the main effort, facilitating control at the most important point of the battlefield. The movement of the command post is influenced by the location of existing wire lines, and the divisional signal officer is kept constantly informed so that communication requirements may be better anticipated. In a delaying action, the commander remains in the forward position until he is convinced that his order for withdrawal is being successfully carried out; then, with his artillery commander, he goes back to the new position. In very difficult or dangerous situations, often present while withdrawals are being executed, the commander will remain with his troops.

General Paulus with his chief of Staff and an aide.

Section II. DUTIES OF THE STAFF

The commander should not be troubled with details. To insure frictionless performances, there are definite assignments to staff positions and duties. Each staff maintains its prescribed strength. The tactical staff remains with the command echelon, whereas the supply and administration staff remains well to the rear, in the vicinity of the trains.

German Troops in Luxemburg.

Section III. ESTIMATE OF THE TERRAIN

Proper utilization of modern implements of war (artillery, airplanes, gas, tanks, etc.) can only be accomplished through their careful adaptation to the terrain. The commander himself can obtain only a general picture of the terrain; he has, however, many supplementary means by which he can learn the true condition of the area in which his command is employed: for example, reconnaissance, air photographs, maps, sketches, and questioning of inhabitants. In judging terrain for specific purposes, you[2] must bear in mind the plan of the commander and the immediate task- — to determine how that plan will be influenced (aided or hindered) by the terrain.

1. ROADS AND ROUTES

Use the best roads available as routes for supply trains; gain protection against air observation, but avoid defiles and narrow valleys. For combat trains, remember that cover from ground observation is also required. How are the roads constructed, and how will bad weather influence them? What are the bad or impossible stretches, and what is the possibility of avoiding or repairing them?

What are the widths?[3] defiles and excavated passages? bridges?[4] fords?[5] ferries?[6] steep grades?[7]

---

[2] The form of the material, here and at many other points, is governed by the fact that it was presented as lectures at the Kriegsakademie.

2. RAILROADS

Differentiate between standard gage (1.435 meters, or 4 feet 8½ inches) and narrow gage (1.20 meters, or 3 feet 11 inches, to 0.6 meter, or 1 foot 11½ inches). Differentiate also between field line, cable line, electric, and steam. How many rails are there, and does room for addition exist alongside the rails? After a small amount of work on the bridges, tracks can usually be adapted for use as marching routes for foot and mounted troops, as well as for motor vehicles.

3. TERRAIN FOR THE ATTACK

(a) Where will the enemy, resist the attack? Where are his advance outposts, main position, switch positions? (6) How has he disposed his forces — infantry, artillery, reserve? (c) Where is a position of

---

[3] For motor vehicles at least 2.5 meters, or 8 feet 4½ inches, and for passing at least 5 meters, or 16 feet 9 inches.
[4] Construction material, capacity, destruction and repair possibilities.
[5] Current speeds, beds, depths (for infantry up to 1 meter, or 3 feet 3.4 inches, for machine guns and heavy infantry weapons up to 0.6 meter, or 1 foot 11.6 inches, and for armored cars up to 0.9 meter or 2 feet 11.4 inches).
[6] Capacity and time required for crossing.
[7] Usually negotiable by motor vehicles if the ratio is not higher than 1 to 7.

readiness (Bereitstellung), and how can the terrain be best utilized for advance to it? Is there concealment from air observation? Until what point will the attacking force be concealed from hostile ground observation? (d) Where are covered approaches for infantry toward the hostile position? Are attack objectives so conspicuous and so located that concentrated artillery fire may be directed upon them? Where are the best positions for artillery and observation posts? Where is the terrain most favorable for tanks? Where does the terrain favor the enemy's counterattack? (e) And, lastly, what kind of attack is most favored by the terrain — penetration, envelopment, or frontal attack?

4. TERRAIN FOR THE DEFENSIVE ACTION

a. *General*

A defensive position is frequently selected through examination of maps. Immediately thereafter, officers are sent on terrain reconnaissance. General Staff, artillery, and engineer officers reconnoiter for their respective purposes or weapons; later, a coordinated defense plan is built up from their information.

b. *Questions To Be Considered*

Such questions as the following arise:

(a) What should be the locations of the main line of resistance, the flank support, the outpost line, and the advance positions? (b) Where can artillery and heavy infantry weapons, as well as their required observation posts, be located to bring the enemy under fire at long ranges? (c) How can the enemy be subjected to frontal and flanking fire immediately in front of the main line of resistance, and where can a counterblow be effectively delivered? (d) What obstacles must be constructed to canalize the attack of the enemy, including his tanks, and to cause him to advance where heavily concentrated fire
can be delivered? (e) Where will the reserves be located to obtain cover and also to facilitate counterattacks? (f) Should it be necessary to limit the enemy's penetration, and how can the defensive be established in a position to the rear?

5. TERRAIN FOR THE DELAYING ACTION

Where is an effective first line of defense? Where are lines of defense to the rear? Where is favorable ground for an outpost line? Where are covered avenues of withdrawal? Where is observation for supporting weapons? Where are natural obstacles and terrain features which can be converted into effective obstacles? Where is terrain which permits long-range observation and firing?

6. TERRAIN FOR THE BIVOUAC

Before the troops arrive, reconnoiter bivouac areas and routes leading thereto. Avoid large assemblages of personnel. The smaller the groups, the easier to conceal in villages, wooded areas, or other suitable locations. Maintain the tactical integrity of units in bivouac. If it is necessary to bivouac by day in open terrain, increase the distance and intervals to minimize the effect of hostile bombing. For tactical purposes, bivouac requirements include: Adequate room; security and screening forces which occupy commanding terrain and are sufficiently strong to permit time and space for the main force to maneuver according to the situation; and routes connecting the various groups and leading to potential defensive areas. Bivouac requirements for troops demand dry ground and land (preferably uncultivated) which is lightly wooded, protected against wind, and convenient to a supply of water, straw, and wood. The proximity of villages is desirable.

A German with a Panzerfaust with camouflage.

Section IV. CONCEALMENT

Troops must use every opportunity and means to deny information to the enemy. Otherwise the essential element in the attack, surprise, is lost. Concealment is most effective when the enemy requires a long time to discover that he has been deceived.

7. PROTECTION AGAINST GROUND RECONNAISSANCE

a. *Hostile Observation*

Hostile observers and staffs can see great distances from high points (observation posts) with field glasses and telescopes; therefore, (a) when troop movements are contemplated, study the map carefully to insure cover against possible hostile observation; (b) conceal movements, positions, and installations by a screen of security forces to the front and flanks.

b. *Offensive Concealment*

Security in all directions must be considered. Concealment may be either offensive or defensive. If offensive, cavalry and other highly mobile combat units are launched against the hostile reconnaissance forces to drive them back. This method is effective, but occasionally hostile patrols are able to infiltrate or go around the attacking force.

c. *Defensive Concealment*

Defensive concealment is particularly effective when the terrain contributes natural obstacles such as a river, a chain of lakes, a swamp, or some similar area. The stronger the natural obstacles, the weaker the force employed to protect the avenues of approach, and also the stronger the force that can be held as mobile reserve. Reconnaissance units are sent far forward, operating energetically and according to opportunity against the hostile reconnaissance force.

d. *False Appearances*

In situations where it is desired to deceive the enemy and impart the impression of great strength, circulate false rumors, execute false marches, and send troops against hostile reconnaissance forces with instructions to fire a great deal of ammunition rapidly, to tie up the hostile communications net, to disturb radio transmission, and to organize deceptive transmission on radio or wire.

8. PROTECTION AGAINST AIR RECONNAISSANCE

Strong activity on the part of the hostile air force requires careful consideration for the concealment of troops and installations, particularly when antiaircraft means are lacking or very limited. The fact that photographs reveal every detail must not be overlooked. Artificial means of concealment, such as camouflage, smoke, or nets, are effective; but it is more important to survey carefully the surrounding area. Avoid constructions and artificial works, sharp color contrasts, and lights. Realize, on the other hand, that measures for concealment hinder the troops, render more difficult, freedom of movement and distribution of orders, and through night marches and detours cause loss of time and decrease the capacity to fight.

9. CONCEALMENT IN REST AREAS

Select rest areas in wooded locations or in several villages. Place horses, tanks, vehicles, etc., under trees or in stalls or courts, but avoid regular parking or parade-ground distribution. Regulate traffic in the area, keeping the main roads and intersections free.

10. CONCEALMENT OF TROOP MOVEMENTS

a. *Loading and Unloading*

In rail movements it is practically impossible to conceal loading and unloading areas from hostile air reconnaissance. When possible, march the troops by night to a village near the loading station, permit them to rest, and then move them on in smaller groups to the village where the loading station is located. Load rapidly and vacate the vicinity promptly.

b. *Road Movements*

In road movements, the concealment given by darkness is most effective. Arrange the departure of troops from bivouac at the beginning of darkness, with arrival in the new area before daybreak. When marching by day, select routes leading through woods, villages, or other partially covered areas. The shadows of trees along the roads offer excellent means for concealing columns, including vehicles. Bridge construction cannot be concealed, but equipment can be so disposed prior to the actual construction that there is little or no tell-tale indication of the preparations.

11. CONCEALMENT IN BATTLE

Carry out development and deployment, or either, under the concealment of darkness. If the situation requires execution by daylight, seek covered areas. Utilize camouflage to conceal the positions of guns, of headquarters, and of observation posts.

A Waffen SS team gathering intelligence.

Section V. COMBAT INTELLIGENCE

The commander must continually, day and night, conduct reconnaissance and utilize intelligence means to seek information clarifying the enemy situation. As soon as possible, he will forward information and important reports to the next higher commander. Once contact with the enemy is gained, steps should be taken not to lose contact. In higher commands, and sometimes with the lower units, a special officer (intelligence officer) will be detailed to handle all intelligence matters. Such an officer works in coordination with all the commanders of attached intelligence units and information services, and keeps them constantly informed of the situation.

12. THE PREPARATION OF INTELLIGENCE REPORTS

Keep in mind the following rules governing the preparation of reports: (a) Determine beforehand what reports must be sent in code and also what means of signal communications are to be used, (b) Differentiate be between what one has personally seen and what another has remarked or reported, (c) Avoid euphemistic phrases and exaggerations, (d) State strength, time, and place exactly, (e) Include information on the condition of the terrain. (f) Send in pertinent information yourself, never assuming that another unit has already sent it in. (g) In very urgent cases, send a report not only to the next higher commander but also direct to the commander-in-chief, (h) From time to time, submit a complete assembly of reports; frequently a sketch will suffice.

13. WHAT TO REPORT

In battle, utilize pauses to send in reports on enemy movements, your own situation, the ammunition supply, the condition of the terrain, and your own impressions. Make suggestions for the seizing of favorable opportunities. Reports giving such information as exists just before darkness sets in are especially valuable. After a battle, report immediately what enemy troops oppose your force, what the enemy is doing, what the condition of your own troops is, where your troops are located, and what the status of the ammunition supply is.

14. CONTACT AND COORDINATION BETWEEN FRIENDLY UNITS

Liaison between neighboring units, and between higher and next lower units, is accomplished through a mutual exchange of reports and a prompt communication of friendly intentions. Large units utilize liaison officers for this purpose, each unit sending one of its officers to the other and holding him responsible for the exchange of information. Such officers keep their commanders informed of the situation with reference to the enemy, all developments of the situation, and the intentions of the other commander. The duties of a liaison officer demand tactical knowledge, intelligence, and tact.

15. TRANSMISSION OF ORDERS AND REPORTS

Several communication means should always be avail- able to a commander. Where technical communication means are uncertain or cannot be maintained, then courier service[8] is established. Very important orders or reports are generally sent by officer messengers in motorcycles or cars. If delivery is uncertain, several means of transmission are used, as well as different routes, to insure the prompt arrival of the information at its destination.

Every commander is required to know the routes of communication and the messenger route. All units assist in the uninterrupted transmission of reports and messages. Higher commanders and commanders of reconnaissance and security units are authorized to examine the messages which they contact en route, noting on the message that they have done so, the hour, and the date.

16. ADVANCE MESSAGE CENTERS

To expedite the receipt of information, advance message centers are established, particularly in the area or sector where communications will be numerous. Such message centers should be easily located,

---

[8] Runners, mounted men, bicyclists, or motorcyclists.

protected from hostile fire, and definitely connected with the rearward message center. Under certain circumstances (for example, on the front of a cavalry corps), advance message centers and message assembly points may be established at considerable distances from the main headquarters, in order to simplify and expedite the transmission of information between the reconnaissance units and the main headquarters.

17. INFORMATION THROUGH SPECIAL MEANS

The air intelligence service observes hostile air activity and provides information relative to the air situation, and from this one can obtain a fairly accurate conception of the enemy's intentions. The signal communication intelligence service observes all hostile communications (radio, telephone, telegraph, etc.) through goniometric intercept listening posts, wire-tapping, observers, and other means. The routine interrogation of prisoners of war yields miscellaneous information. Captured documents may include orders, maps, messages, notebooks, newspapers, photographs, and films. Scrutiny of the hostile press and publications is maintained.

18. IMPORTANT PRINCIPLES OF RECONNAISSANCE

Do not dissipate reconnaissance strength. Superiority of means is very important for successful reconnaissance; but superiority in mobility and clever employment tend to offset numerical inferiority. It will frequently be necessary to fight for information. Advanced hostile security and reconnaissance forces must be penetrated or thrown back to make contact possible with the hostile main force. In this connection, it is often advisable to occupy important points quickly with motorized forces. When there is great inferiority to the enemy, fighting should be avoided, and an endeavor should be made to penetrate the enemy screen or go around it.

The commander who specifies what information is to be obtained should coordinate all his subordinate reconnaissance means. Efficient reconnaissance is not obtained through employment of large numbers of reconnoitering units, but by the careful direction and instruction of these units as to what the commander wishes to know. Definite missions and their relative urgency, must be indicated, and the means of sending information to the rear, including definitely regulated radio traffic, must be insured.

19. STRATEGIC RECONNAISSANCE

Strategic, or operative, reconnaissance endeavors to build up a general picture of the overall situation, thus aiding the commander in chief in making the decisions which have important influence on the entire campaign.

Missions may include observation of hostile mobilizations, assemblies, initial march directions, railroad movements, boat movements, supply echelons, construction of fortifications, air activities, locations, strengths, movements of motorized and mechanized forces, and, particularly, open flanks. Such missions are performed by air reconnaissance units, motorized reconnaissance battalions, and army cavalry units. The three must supplement each other and be carefully coordinated to that end.

20. TACTICAL RECONNAISSANCE

Tactical reconnaissance is concerned with the movements of the enemy in closer proximity: his movements, bivouac areas, organization, breadth and depth of disposition, supply service, construction of defensive works, air activity, and location of airfields and antiaircraft. Especially important is timely report of the location of motorized or mechanized forces.

For air reconnaissance, the commander utilizes the air-plane squadron which is placed at his disposal for such purpose by the air force. For ground reconnaissance, he utilizes independent motorized reconnaissance battalions, motorized reconnaissance battalions of the cavalry, mounted reconnaissance battalions of the cavalry, and reconnaissance battalions of the infantry divisions.

21. RECONNAISSANCE BATTALIONS

Definite sectors are generally assigned to reconnaissance battalions. Within the corps, boundaries between divisions are designated, and on open flanks the boundary is designated between the flank reconnaissance area of the division and that of the corps. Reconnaissance units avoid fighting unless it is absolutely required by the situation in the accomplishment of their missions. If a reconnaissance unit be given a security mission, the unit should be reinforced by others units: for example, by machine gun, light artillery, antitank, and engineer troops.

If a reconnaissance battalion is directly in front of the division and in contact with the enemy, it should be ordered either: (a) to move off to a side and continue reconnaissance in that area, or (b) to await relief from troops coming up from the rear, or (c) to fall back upon the troops in the rear. In the absence of any orders, under the aforesaid circumstances the reconnaissance battalion should fall back upon the troops in the rear. On an open flank, reconnaissance battalions are echeloned forward.

22. MOTORIZED RECONNAISSANCE BATTALIONS

The important advantage is speed. Motorized reconnaissance battalions can reconnoiter by day and march on by night, and are restricted only by limitations of the motor vehicles, terrain, weather, roads, fuel supply, and signal communication. They maintain connection with mounted reconnaissance units by radio. Advancing forward by bounds — the nearer the enemy, the shorter the bounds — they remain as long as possible on roads. In hostile territory, different routes for the return are selected, and important points along the road, or important places, are secured. Rest during the night is obtained by avoiding main roads and villages, and by halting under available cover in isolated areas. Contact with the enemy, however, must be maintained.

The width of a sector should not be over 50 kilometers (31 miles). The depth is limited by fuel supply. Motor vehicles in modern reconnaissance units have a radius of action of between 200 to 250 kilometers (125 to 155 miles) without replenishment.

Scouting groups will generally be organized and dispatched by the commander of a battalion. Such groups include armored scout cars, motorcycles, and radio equipment. Along the more important roads and those leading to the decisive areas or points, patrols should be stronger, but too large a patrol increases the difficulty of concealment from the enemy. Armored car patrols within scouting groups will be given written orders pertaining to route, destination, and information desired; they advance by bounds, with distance and speed sometimes prescribed; generally, however, they precede the division at about 1 hour (approximately 40 kilometers, or 25 miles). Motorcycles are used to fill in gaps and intervals, thereby thickening the reconnaissance net. The remainder of the motorized reconnaissance battalion serves as a reserve and as a receiving and assembly point for reports.

23. RECONNAISSANCE BATTALION OF THE INFANTRY DIVISION

The reconnaissance battalion of the infantry division is employed as a unit, even if the division is advancing over a broad front in several columns. The advance is made by bounds somewhat shorter than those of the motorized reconnaissance battalion. Scout groups are sent out under the direction of the battalion commander. The battalion can reconnoiter an area approximately 10 kilometers (6 miles) in width, and seldom is sent more than 30 or 40 kilometers (25 to 30 miles) forward. The strength of the scout groups (sometimes up to that of a platoon with light machine guns) is, however, determined by the situation and the mission. Patrols sent out from the scout groups remain on the roads as long as possible, advancing by bounds from observation point to observation point.

Reconnaissance battalions of interior divisions are usually withdrawn to the rear after the battle actually begins. If, however, the division is operating over a broad front or in difficult terrain, the battalion may be reinforced, and utilized to fill in a gap or to seize an important terrain feature. Communications must be carefully provided. Extra signal equipment and personnel may be attached in exceptional cases.

24. BATTLE RECONNAISSANCE

The purpose of battle reconnaissance is to reconnoiter the enemy's front, flanks, and rear to establish definitely the location of his flanks, artillery, heavy infantry weapons, and reserves. Such reconnaissance locates our own front line and often provides close-in security and terrain reconnaissance.[9] Security is necessary at all times, but reconnaissance must not be neglected to accomplish security. Battle reconnaissance is established usually at the opening phases of the development or deployment. The advance of the infantry in the attack reveals very quickly the location of hostile infantry and artillery, also, fire from our artillery upon hostile infantry will generally result in the hostile artillery delivering counter-fire and thus revealing its location.

There are both air and ground means available for performing battle reconnaissance. Some of the specific means of battle reconnaissance are: (a) Infantry patrols, sometimes reinforced with light machine guns, heavy

---

[9] Our observation posts and other friendly personnel, who are reconnoitering for our own artillery, heavy infantry weapon, and antitank positions, can gain much helpful information from units of the reconnaissance battalion. Sometimes they actually accompany the battalion to get early information about the terrain, potential targets, and gun positions.

machine guns, light mortars, or antitank guns, (b) Engineer patrols, particularly valuable in approaching a fortified area, a defile, or a river, (c) Artillery patrols, consisting usually of an officer and a few mounted men assigned to reconnoiter routes of approach, observation posts, and fire positions, (d) Observation battalion (artillery), skilled in locating targets by sound and flash, and in evaluating aerial photographs.[10] (e) Captive balloons, supplementing the preceding means and permitting a general view over the hostile front.

------

[10] It assists our own artillery in firing on concealed targets by transmitting weather data. By accurate surveying principles, it establishes the location net for the batteries. The net is not restricted to the division sector, but sometimes extends 6 to 10 kilometers (as much as 6 miles).

A German soldier with a dog, possibly used for messaging.

Section VI. PRINCIPLES OF COMMUNICATION

The higher unit is responsible for the establishment and maintenance of communication with the next lower unit. Wire connection with neighboring units is always established to the unit on the right. This rule does not release the commanders of responsibility, however, to maintain contact with units to their left.

Of special importance is the connection between artillery and infantry. If an artillery unit is attached to an infantry unit, then the infantry is responsible for the connection; if the artillery is supporting an infantry unit, but not attached to it, then the artillery is responsible for the connection. If, however, the artillery, through some special circumstances, is unable to establish the connection, then the infantry must undertake the responsibility. Connection with heavy infantry weapons is the responsibility of the infantry commander concerned.

25. OPERATION OF SIGNAL COMMUNICATION TROOPS

The commander issues orders for the employment of his communication units ordinarily after receiving the recommendations of the communication officer. It is most essential that the commander punctually give the communication officer a complete picture of the situation, including the commander's intentions. The communication means of a command post are assembled in a message center. The proper functioning of communication is dependent upon its useful employment on the part of the commander and upon the technical training of personnel.

26. ORDER OF THE DIVISION COMMUNICATION OFFICER

The order of the division communication officer should contain: (a) The enemy situation, our own troops, the plan of the commander; (b) the mission of the signal battalion; (c) specific orders for the signal communication companies and supply train; (d) when applicable, instructions relative to secrecy, replacement, utilization of commercial nets, and system maintenance.

In the advance march, the division communication battalion builds and maintains an axis of signal communication (wire lines) along the route upon which the division commander and his headquarters are advancing. In friendly territory, the existing commercial net is utilized to a maximum; in enemy territory, heavy field cable is generally installed overhead. When contact with the enemy has been established by the division, wire communication must be maintained at all costs with the corps and must also be supplemented by radio and other means. Establishment of lateral connections within the division and between divisions is also very important in coordinating the tactical effort.

Within the division, all command posts and observation posts should be connected according to their relative importance. The division signal battalion will establish lines to the infantry regiments, artillery commander, and the artillery units operating under the artillery commander, as well as lateral connection to adjoining divisions. When there is a deficiency of means, the establishment of the aforementioned artillery connection has priority. The division signal officer will coordinate the establishment of the communication net and supervise its construction by his own signal troops and the communication troops of the various units. In a rapidly advancing attack, in pursuit, or in withdrawals or retreat, he will restrict the amount of installation,

27. COMMUNICATION IN THE DEFENSE

In the defense a very extensive communication net is established. Its construction is governed by the situation, and by the time, materiel, and personnel available. Several means of communication between all important defensive installations are provided. Wire communication is carried by buried cables. Special communication nets (such as infantry, artillery, anti-aircraft) are established. Alarms for gas and air attacks are installed. Technical means to intercept hostile messages are intensified.

28. VARIOUS MEANS OF COMMUNICATION

When new troops are attached to a command, additional communication requirements are introduced; so reserve communication personnel should always be held out. The operation of communication troops must not be interfered with in any manner by other units. The various means of communication can be characterized as follows:

(a) *Telephone.* — Installation of the telephone requires time and materiel. Wire lines are sensitive to such disturbances as fire, wind, snow, frost, and storms. The enemy can easily listen in on conversations, particularly over single-wire connections; in the danger zone, therefore, double lines and heavy insulated wires are used.

(b) *Telegraph.* — The telegraph is simple in operation and installation, and very often cannot be easily intercepted. The Morse code is utilized.

(c) *Automobile, mounted messenger, bicyclist, motorcyclist, runner.* — In a war of movement, these means are often the most reliable. They are used without hesitancy when technical means are not available. Speeds of transmission vary.[11]

(d) *Radio.* — When wire connections fail or are not functioning steadily, the radio is indispensable. Electric storms, static, other radio transmission on similar wave lengths, mountains, and other interferences minimize effective range of hearing. In practice, radio is valuable only if messages are short; transmissions should therefore be in telegram form, omitting all unessential words.

(e) *Blinker.* — This is an important signal means in battle when wire lines are destroyed. It cannot be used for great distances, and is greatly restricted by fog, mist, bright sunshine, or proximity of enemy observation. Blinker messages must be very short, since 20 words require about 10 minutes for transmission.

(f) *Rockets, Very lights, flares.* — These serve as signals whose meaning has been prearranged and is thoroughly understood by the troops concerned. Very pistols and pyrotechnic equipment are carried

---

[11] Messenger on horse, 1 kilometer (3/8ths mile) in 5 to 7 minutes; automobile or motorcycle, 30 to 40 kilometers (25 to 31 miles) per hour — on good roads considerably faster; bicyclist, 15 to 20 kilometers (12 to 15 miles) per hour.

habitually on light telephone carts and also in all combat trains. Ability to see these signal lights is greatly influenced by the terrain. Also, there is always the chance of confusion with enemy signal lights.

(g) *Signal flags and panels.* – Prearranged signals with these means enable ground troops to send short messages, particularly in communicating with airplanes and balloons.

(h) *Alarms.* — Horns, sirens, bells, and gongs are used for gas or hostile airplane warning.

(i) *Signal gun.* — This small mortar, which projects a message container, is useful in position warfare.

(j) *Courier pigeons.* — Although requiring at least 3 days to orient, courier pigeons are useful under heavy fire, for they are sensitive to gas, and terrain does not influence them. They fly about 1 kilometer (5/8ths mile) in a minute. They do not fly in darkness, rain, or storm, and with snow it is difficult for them to orient themselves.

(k) *Message dogs.* — Expert and affectionate care by the men in charge of message dogs results in most satisfactory returns. Such dogs can be used under heavy fire, and can remember and find locations on a battlefield in a radius of about 2 kilometers (1¼ miles). They will efficiently follow an artificially made track (scent) up to 6 kilometers (about 4 miles).

(l) *Listening-in apparatus.* — This apparatus is established to determine the location of hostile activity in planting mines, and to listen in on hostile communications.

(m) *Airplanes.* — An airplane may be used to connect a division headquarters with its foremost elements or neighbor units. In such cases, no other reconnaissance mission should be given the plane. It is important to establish the location of the foremost line of infantry and of the hostile line; the infantry troops on prearranged signal will display panels to assist the plane on the mission. Planes may be used for artillery fire direction, and for maintaining connection between division, cavalry division, and corps or army headquarters. They are particularly adapted to distributing quickly important orders or delivering reports to units a considerable distance away.

(n) *Captive balloons.* — Balloons observe artillery fire, give prearranged signals indicating the time of the day, the signal to open fire, etc. Their communication means include flags, panels, blinkers, and telephones. Weather conditions, heavy-wooded terrain, and mountainous country restrict their usefulness.

German troops on the move in Stalingrad.

Section VII. ESTIMATE OF THE SITUATION

You must thoroughly work yourself into the situation. Place upon the situation map the location of your own troops and put down the information that you have about the enemy. This information is built up by reports from various sources, as suggested above under the heading "Combat Intelligence." Information must be evaluated objectively; one must be extremely careful not to interpret what is received as one would like it to be, or as one hoped it would be. A large part of the information received in war is contradictory, a still greater part is false, and by far the greatest part is very uncertain.

29. GUIDING PRINCIPLES

Carefully read the orders received from the next higher commander, and consider all information received. In considering the situation, the following principles govern: The first and most important principle is to utilize to the maximum the available means. Any moderation in this regard is a deterring factor in attaining the ultimate goal. Second, concentrate as much of your force as possible where you plan or believe the principal blow (the main effort) will fall, and expose yourself disadvantageously at other points, in order to be more certain of success at the point of the main effort. The success of the main effort more than compensates for any minor losses sustained. Third, lose no time. Unless special advantages accrue by delay, it is very important that you execute your plans as quickly as possible; through speedy action many measures of the enemy are nullified in their initial stages. Finally, you must weigh each situation independently, restricting yourself only to a consideration of the essentials. The following questions may here occur:

Mission. — What is my mission? Does it require decisive action or delaying action? Must I fight an independent action or will I be influenced by the movements or action of other troops?

Terrain. — What is the condition of terrain between my troops and the enemy? Which routes lead toward the enemy? Where does the terrain permit approaches covered from air or land observation for an attack on the enemy position? When my mission requires defense, where does the terrain offer favorable defensive positions? What possibilities are therefore available for the fulfillment of my mission?

Enemy. — What can the enemy do to counter my plans? Where is the enemy now located?[12] Are there any bases for his strength and organization? What can he do, making correct tactical suppositions?[13] Are there any indications that the enemy has acted incorrectly? Do I know anything about the ability or personality of the commander or the condition of his troops? How will the terrain influence the enemy's action? How can I best fulfill my mission with the most damage to the enemy?

Own troops. — Where are my own troops? Which are immediately available? Which troops can be later drawn in? And when? Are special transportation means such as a railroad or motor trucks at my disposal? What

---

[12] Always favor the enemy in computing the distances possibly covered by the enemy since his position was last reported.
[13] Always assume that he will carry out his plan most disadvantageously to you.

can I expect from my troops considering their past performance? How is the supply situation, especially with regard to ammunition? Is support from other organizations possible? Which of the present possible solutions will give the greatest success?

30. CHANGING THE MISSION

As a result of all these considerations, is the accomplishment of my mission no longer possible? (When, owing to unavoidable circumstances or unpredictable events, it is impossible to carry out a mission, then and then only may I change my mission, and I must then assume full responsibility for the change. I must select a substitute mission to assist effectively the general scheme of maneuver. I must notify at once the next higher commander in case I decide that it is impossible to carry out my assigned mission.)

31. SEIZING THE INITIATIVE

In general, when confronted by a vague situation and difficult circumstances, as is often the case in war — be active. Seize and maintain the initiative. Do not expect or await hints or suggestions from the enemy relative to your next move.

German troops at the battle of Kursk.

Section VIII. THE DECISION

The decision must indicate a clear objective to be attained by the coordinated and aggressive use of available means. The strong will of the leader must dominate at all times; often the stronger will compels victory. Never let anxiety over personal security interfere or influence in any manner the real task, which is the annihilation of the enemy. Calmly weigh the situation, thinking quickly but overlooking nothing essential. Insure that all assistants clearly understand your plans. Nervousness on your part is quickly reflected by subordinates.

Never hold a council of war. Complication and confusion are frequently introduced, and generally only an incomplete decision results. One can think through a situation much better and reach a definite decision by independently estimating the situation.[14]

Once a decision is made, do not deviate, except for excellent reasons. In this connection, however, one can bring about disaster by obstinately clinging to the initial decision when justifiable grounds are present for a change. The true art of leadership is the ability to recognize when a new decision is required by the developments or changes in the situation. The commander should be resolute but not obstinate.

---

[14] The division commander will generally hear the suggestions and proposals of his chief of staff.

A German officer directing the construction of a barricade in Stalingrad.

Section IX. FIELD ORDERS

Publishing orders is an art that can be learned only by continual practice. Prompt distribution of faultless orders furthers the confidence of the troops in the leader and often has decisive influence in achieving success in combat. Conversely, power in the attack or strength to resist in the defense can be greatly reduced by faulty orders.

Commanders of divisions or larger units generally use written orders. Simple instructions and brief missions may be communicated orally or through the communications net, but the text should be simultaneously recorded. Commanders of units smaller than a division generally use oral orders, but again, the text must be recorded in writing. While higher commanders usually make reference to points or areas on maps, commanders of small units point out or make such designations actually on the terrain. Although oral discussions with subordinates may contribute to clarity, the leader should not become dependent upon such discussions. Decisions and orders remain the direct responsibility of the leader himself.

32. GENERAL RULES

The following rules embrace accepted fundamentals and help to gain uniformity: (a) Do not issue orders until your plan of action is definitely established. (b) Distribute the order early enough to allow the lower echelons time for further dissemination and full compliance. (c) Create conditions that are conducive to clearness and conciseness, leaving nothing to mutual agreements. (d) Place yourself mentally in the shoes of the subordinates receiving the order, (e) State only what subordinates must know for the proper performance of their tasks. (f) Always state definitely whether the combat is to be attack, delaying action, or defense, and whether the troops must remain "prepared for action" or whether they "may rest." (g) Issue affirmative statements, avoiding ambiguous or vague expressions and statements of exaggeration.[15] (h) Include a brief commendation of a unit for the execution of a difficult or unusual task, particularly when, troops are ordered to withdraw, to retire, or to pursue under circumstances difficult for the troops to comprehend, (i) Use prescribed abbreviations, (j) Embody pertinent information for each subject, unit, or weapon in a separate paragraph, underlining key words or phrases, (k) Number all orders successively, also the paragraphs within the order.

33. WARNING ORDERS (VORBEFEHLE)

Warning orders, usually transmitted orally, by telephone, or by radio, are issued to troops to give advance information about the will of the commander. The information contained therein is influenced by existing circumstances — the time available, the situation with respect to the enemy and our own troops, etc. — but in general will include such items as the plan of the commander, arrangements for reconnaissance and security, time and place of departures, march destination, bivouacs, halts, and changes of direction-

---

[15] A statement of conjecture or expectation must be definitely stated as such.

Warning orders must be followed as soon as practicable by a complete order or an individual order.

34. COMPLETE OPERATIONS ORDERS (GESAMTBEFEHLE)

Complete operations orders present a full survey of the situation with respect to the enemy and our troops, the plan of the commander, the role each unit will play, and pertinent information for the troops. The usual arrangement follows:

Enemy. — Pertinent information of the enemy, including strength, dispositions, condition, losses sustained, defeats suffered, and the commander's expectation of what the enemy may do.

Own troops. — A brief orientation involving the next higher units, neighboring units, and special supporting units.

General plan. — A clear and concise expression of the plan of the commander (not repetition of the plan of the next higher commander), to ensure that subordinates fully understand his intentions.

Detailed plan. — An announcement of the specific details relating to such matters as reconnaissance, missions, supply and evacuation, communication, and the command post.[16]

35. SEPARATE ORDERS (EINZELBEFEHLE)

Separate orders (Einzelbefehle) are issued when circumstances render it impractical or unnecessary to issue a complete operations order (Gesamtbefehl). Such circumstances include situations wherein individual units must be given specific or special instructions, or where the time available does not permit the issuance of a complete operations order. The separate order (Einzelbefehl) contains the necessary information to insure coordination of effort; and later the publication of the complete field order will include such information, briefly stated, as was sent out previously in individual orders.

36. SPECIAL INSTRUCTIONS (BESONDERE ANORDNUNGEN)

---

[16] As to reconnaissance, the detailed plan mentions the enemy information desired, the areas to be reconnoitered and by whom and when, the time and place where resulting reports are to be sent, and the sequence of reconnaissances according to their urgency. As to missions, what each unit with indicated attachments or detachments must fulfill is clearly stated. In respect to supply and evacuation, the definite functioning of agencies in relation to the combat elements is specified. As regards communication, the axis of communication for the unit publishing the order is indicated, and special instructions, such as those pertaining to the use of the radio or existing commercial nets, are included. As for the command post, the location of the commander's headquarters and the tune when it opens or closes, etc., are given.

Special instructions supplement operations orders with information principally concerning ammunition, communication, equipment, food supply, transportation, medical and veterinary service, construction, and civil population. In general, special instructions are written and are issued direct to the units or agencies that they concern.

German troops on the move in Stalingrad.

Section X. MARCHES

All arrangements pertaining to a march should be based upon the premise that the mass of the force must arrive at the new destination with the minimum effort and the maximum secrecy. When contact with the enemy is imminent, the march formation should favor easy and rapid development for combat. When contact is unlikely, the comfort of the command is the important consideration. In view of modem air developments, movements under cover of darkness will be the rule rather than the exception. There will be circumstances requiring day marches, however; or they may be safely undertaken when the weather precludes hostile air activity.

37. MARCHING IN MULTIPLE COLUMNS

The command should be marched in multiple columns, using all available routes, thereby saving the strength of the troops, affording better protection against air attacks, and maintaining the command in such formation as to facilitate development for combat. The following considerations, however, prevail: (a) Organization in depth permits freedom of maneuver. (b) Echelonment of some columns on the open flank affords protection or facilitates later envelopment of the hostile flank when the enemy is fixed in the front, (c) The strength of columns and the location of stronger columns will be determined by the whereabouts of the enemy and by the tactical plan, as influenced by the terrain, (d) If the situation is initially too vague to determine such dispositions, then several weak columns should be marched into aggressive action against the enemy to clarify the situation; the mass of the force may then follow in one or more columns, (e) The width of the advance should not be so broad as to preclude the building up of a main effort when contact with the enemy is made. (f) Zones of advance with boundaries should be indicated, (g) And, lastly, transmission of orders and reports must be carefully organized.

38. MARCHING IN SINGLE COLUMN

The division sometimes cannot avoid marching in a single column. The great disadvantage is the extraordinary length, which precludes assembling for a coordinated effort in 1 day. An advantage of the single column over multiple columns is greater security and flexibility for changing direction.

39. PROTECTION AGAINST AIR ATTACKS

The movements of large forces are protected by anti- aircraft precautions, particularly at initial points, river crossings, and defiles. Antiaircraft batteries advancing by bounds are set out in advance to front and flanks to provide protection at these critical points. The commander must insure that antiaircraft units have priority on roads. The danger from air attacks during daylight is greatly reduced by the following appropriate methods:

Increasing the depth of march columns — At the command Fliegermarschtiefel (air defense depth), the troop units, horse-drawn elements, and other vehicles double the distances normally maintained on the march. Simultaneously it is indicated whether security forces, such as flank or advance guards, maintain, increase, or decrease distances. Arrangements are made for air defense depth, if circumstances require such precaution, at the beginning of the march; or rest periods may be used to increase or decrease distances. With short march columns, extension or retraction are also accomplished during the march.

Increasing the breadth of march columns. — At the command Fliegermarschbreitel (air defense breadth), the troops spread out, using both sides of a highway or even expanding into the adjacent fields. The formation invariably imposes march difficulties upon the troops and is avoided whenever possible. When troops are already marching in air defense depth, it is seldom necessary to require the additional precaution of marching in air defense breadth.

Dividing a column. — Very long columns marching along a single route are broken up into several short groups with between 1- and 3-kilometer (1- to 2-mile) intervals.

Disposing of the motorized units. — The motorized units of the infantry division, except the reconnaissance battalion or units employed on security missions, are divided into groups and follow the various columns, advancing by bounds. If the situation permits, they are organized into a motorized column and marched on a special road. Motor vehicles are also marched in the intervals between the advance guard and the main body, and between units of the main body.

Averting hostile planes. — Upon the approach of hostile planes, air guards promptly sound the warning, using pre-arranged signals. Marching troops throw themselves down on, or off to the sides of, the road. Motor vehicles halt, and their drivers set the brakes. Mounted troops clear the road and continue the march under available cover. Antiaircraft weapons immediately fire upon' the hostile planes, but riflemen do not fire unless a plane comes within range. Frequently the troops are put in readiness to withstand a simultaneous air and gas attack. At night, if flares are employed by the hostile fliers, foot soldiers throw themselves to the ground off the roadside. Everyone else and all vehicles remain absolutely motionless while antiaircraft artillery provides defense.

40. NIGHT MARCHES

Although night marches initially tax the strength of troops, this disadvantage is minimized after troops become adjusted to resting in day .bivouacs and eating regularly on a changed schedule. Night marches have decided advantages: they deny altogether or restrict materially hostile ground and air reconnaissance, and by keeping the enemy ignorant, they contribute to surprise; also, night marches bring troops into position for battle with fewer losses and consequently higher morale.

In spite of the fact that main highways are often illuminated with flares by hostile aviators, it is frequently necessary to utilize highways for marches. If many alternative parallel routes are available, the principal highways are avoided, or utilized by motor elements only.

The hour of assembly at the beginning of the march should come after dark in order to preclude observation by hostile planes. Troops are formed as for a day march without extension of distance or expansion of width for air defense; but the security forces are drawn in somewhat closer, and distances between units are slightly increased to insure sufficient buffer room. Double connecting files; sent by the principal unit to the subordinate unit, or from the rear unit to the forward unit, are liberally used to maintain contact. The order of march is similar to the arrangement for a day march. If the tactical situation permits, foot troops precede the mounted troops.

On good roads and by starlight or moonlight, the rate of march is practically the same as that of a day march. On poor roads or in heavy darkness, the rate decreases to 3 kilometers (just under 2 miles) per hour and even less. Bicycle troops and motorized units also march appreciably slower by night than by day. It is advisable to arrange short rests — about 10 minutes in every hour; long rest periods tend to make the troops sleepy.

The alert commander does not march his troops directly into bivouac if daylight is about to arrive. He halts them in an available covered area and arranges to have them divided into small groups before the troops march on to bivouac or other destination.

41. DAY MARCHES

When contact with the enemy is at all possible, the commander must march his command during the day with "preparedness for combat" as the foremost consideration. When contact with the enemy is not imminent, the commander can divide his command and march the various units on several routes. When time is not pressing, the movement also can be carried out in small groups over long periods of time. In any case, the first consideration in a day march is tactical; but the possibilities of cover should not be overlooked. The stronger columns should be marched over the routes offering the most cover, while the weaker can be sent over the more open routes. The time of departure on a day march is influenced by the situation, the weather, the season, the length of the intended march, the condition of the troops, and other factors. It is desirable to march from an old bivouac area under cover of darkness and reach a new one by daylight.

42. ORGANIZATION FOR MARCHING

Infantry marches in columns of three men abreast, cavalry marches in columns of two abreast (exceptionally four), and motor vehicles travel in single columns. In general the right side of the road is used; but when organizations are mixed, the infantry should be permitted to march on the more comfortable side for walking. Within the infantry division, the commander must organize his troops for the march so that he can bring all of them to bear against the enemy in a concerted attack in a single day. In order to accomplish this, it may be necessary to march in two, three, or four columns, with each column providing its own security. Examples are illustrated by the following diagrams:

Example 1 (Where the division is marching in columns a, b, and c, and there are no adjacent units)

Example 2 (Where the division is marching with its left flank open)

Example 3 (Where the division is marching as an interior unit)

Example 4 (Where there is a containing Force and the division is marching as an enveloping force)

43. CONNECTION AND COMMUNICATION

The commander of a larger unit is responsible for connection with the next lower; the smaller units must cooperate, however, when difficulties arise. In terrain, or under circumstances, where visibility is restricted, arrangements for continuous connection are intensified. On a march in several columns, communication between the columns is maintained through the most appropriate available means.[17]

44. RATES OF MARCH

---

[17] Airplanes (troops expose panels upon signal from the air observer), radio (when secrecy does not preclude its use), ray lamps, liaison officers (through the messenger system), wire telephone and telegraph (when contact with the enemy is imminent), blinker (frequently), and signal flags (seldom).

Since it is important to provide conditions which permit an even rate of march, the mixing of different sorts of troops should be avoided as much as possible.[18] On good roads and under favorable conditions the following average speeds can be accomplished:[19]

Troops	Per Hour
Foot Troops	5 km (3 mi)
Foot Troops (Small Units)	6 km (3½ mi)
Mounted Troops (Trot and Walk)	7 km (4 mi)
Mounted Troops (Trot)	10 km (6 mi)
Bicyclists	12 km (7½ mi)
Motorcyclists	40 km (25 mi)

Large organizations with all weapons:

(1) Including rest periods 4 km (2½ mi)

(2) Under stress, without rest periods 5 km (3 mi)

Motorized units 30 km (18 mi)

---

[18] Pack animals are one disturbing factor in maintaining an even rate of march.

[19] For foot troops under ordinary conditions the distance prescribed as a "buffer" between companies, or similar units, is 10 paces; for mounted troops and trains, 15 paces. Such distances do not apply, of course, when air defense depth has been ordered.

Intense heat, poor roads, snow, ice, absence of bridges, and other local conditions greatly influence the march rate and the travel distance accomplished. The rate for foot troops on a cross-country or mountainous march decreases from the normal hourly rate by as much as 2 or 3 kilometers.

When great distances must be covered rapidly, motor and rail transportation can be used to expedite marches; for distances under 150 kilometers (93 miles) the use of motor transportation is recommended. When circumstances require foot or mounted troops to make forced marches, every effort is made to assist the accomplishment. Strict march discipline is preserved, and severe measures are meted out against malingerers. The men are told why the particular march is being made, and arrangements are made for rests where refreshments such as hot coffee or tea will be served. Their packs are carried, if possible, in trains.

45. MARCH RESTS

The commander should indicate in the march order all the necessary information concerning the duration and other conditions of the march. An officer should be sent forward to reconnoiter suitable areas for rests. Arrangements should be made for a short halt, not longer than 15 minutes, to begin after the troops have marched about 2 kilometers (1½ miles) so that equipment and clothing may be comfortably readjusted on the men and animals. The troops remain near the road during such short periods, spreading out only a sufficient distance to secure cover from hostile air observation. When a long march is made, halts are ordered about every 2 hours. Rest periods are utilized for eating, drinking, feeding animals, and checking vehicles. The stopping places should be near water and not too restricted. In summer a rest should be prescribed during the hottest time of the day. During long rest periods the troops are arranged in groups; and when hostile airplanes approach, the air guards sound the warning and the troops take cover, remaining motionless.

46. MARCH OUTPOSTS

The security of a force in a rest area is obtained by careful preparation within the area and by sending out security forces instructed to conduct reconnaissances, these cautions being exercised in order to prevent the enemy from obtaining information about the main force, and in order to protect the main force from surprise and give it time to prepare for combat.

According to the degree of danger, if far from the enemy, simpler precautions may be taken; but since the effect of distance has been greatly reduced by motorization and air operations, the following principles of out posting should apply.

(a) Employ the minimum number of troops consistent with the situation, (b) Exploit the natural protective features of the terrain, particularly if the enemy is liable to employ armored vehicles; always establish road blocks, (c) By day, maintain observers in points of vantage for distant viewing of the surrounding terrain, (d) By night, maintain listening points and patrols on or near all possible avenues of approach, (e) Provide protection for the flanks and rear. (f) Establish air guards and a warning system.

German infantry moving through Stalingrad.

Section XI. VARIOUS TYPES OF BATTLE

The most important types of battle are the attack, the defense, and the withdrawal, or retreat. A combination of these types occurs simultaneously or successively in the course of every major campaign. The commander and the General Staff Officer must master the fundamental principles involved in these various forms of tactical maneuver. Resolute application of these principles may penetrate, at least will help to neutralize; the ever-present "fog of war."

German infantry and armor in Stalingrad.

Section XII. THE ATTACK

The attack may be launched (a) from one direction against front, flank, or rear; (b) from several directions simultaneously; (c) after penetration, into a new direction.

47. FORMS OF ATTACK

The frontal attack is the most frequent form of attack, but mechanized and motorized weapons will decrease this frequency. It requires superiority in strength and produces decisive results only when the hostile front is penetrated.

The enveloping attack (envelopment) is the most effective form of maneuver, and if aggressively employed deep in the hostile flank or rear, it can result in a most decisive victory, or even annihilation of the enemy. An envelopment of both flanks presumes marked superiority in means. Wide envelopments are more effective than close-in. Among the factors that contribute to successful envelopments are deception, concentration of strength at the critical point, available reserves, mobility, and simplicity of maneuver. As to surprise, the enemy must not be given the time necessary to take countermeasures. As to mass, strength must be concentrated on the flank of the envelopment so that hostile extension of the line can be overrun or circumvented, and hostile defensive moves quickly and effectively frustrated. As to fixing the enemy, the hostile forces in the front must be contained simultaneously with the enveloping attack.[20]

The penetration is an attack where the maneuver is intended to split or separate the hostile line of

---

[20] This may be accomplished by point attack (which is both effective, and economical in troops), by frontal attack (which involves employment of considerable force and thereby reduces the troops available for the main effort), and by attack with limited objective, (which requires a smaller force and releases more troops for the main effort).

resistance. The following considerations contribute to success: selection of a favorable point (a weak part of the enemy position, or favorable terrain); surprise (such as feints at other points, or secrecy in concentration of strength); breadth of penetration (preferable a base as wide as the depth of the penetration or wider); depth in organization (to exploit breaking through, and to check hostile counter-attacks); rapid and full exploitation of the break-through.

The limited objective attack is a form of maneuver intended to win important terrain features, to contain the enemy frontally, or to stop the hostile advance. Organization in depth is not required.

48. CONSIDERATIONS FOR AN ATTACK

Some important general considerations for an attack are the following: (a) Obtain unity of command and action; avoid piecemeal attacks, (b) Establish a main effort, (c) Assign narrow zones of action, (d) Reinforce fire by additional artillery and heavy infantry weapons, (e) Coordinate and intensify the fire of all weapons, (f) Make timely employment of tanks and reserves, (g) Exploit successes quickly and fully even though the location of the main effort may properly have to be changed.[21] (h) Recognize the crisis in a battle and react appropriately.

Be alert to every advantage, to each success no matter how small, to any mistakes made by the enemy — and exploit these to the fullest degree. If the attack appears definitely stopped by strong hostile resistance at a certain point, further success may be better accomplished by injecting fresh troops, by concentrating fires on a different area, or by changing the disposition of troops.

49. MECHANICS OF ATTACK

The width of a zone of action is dependent upon terrain and mission. A battalion of infantry with both flanks protected is assigned a zone of action 400 to 1,000 meters (roughly 440 to 1,100 yards) wide. An infantry division in a meeting engagement where terrain is favorable for employment of supporting weapons, is assigned a zone of action 4,000 to 5,000 meters (4,400 to 5,500 yards) wide; but an infantry division having both flanks protected and making the main effort against a strong hostile position is assigned a zone of action of 3,000 meters (3,281 yards).

---

[21] For example, in passing an obstacle — river or mountain chain — the main effort may be switched during the progress of the operation, because of a break-through in an unexpected point.

A definite objective or direction must be indicated for the attack. Although zones of action are prescribed, they need not be completely filled with troops. For divisions and larger units, these zones are selected from the map; for the smaller units, they are determined by inspection of the terrain itself. The boundaries are extended deep enough into hostile territory to preclude mixing of units for the duration of the day's operation. Strongpoints and difficult terrain must be included within a unit's zone of action and not located on its boundary line. Frequently only the designation of an objective is required in order to maintain direction and to preclude mixing of organizations.

Do not include too much detail in the attack order and thus restrict initiative. The mission must be clear — what to do, but not how to do it.

The important task of all weapons is to enable the infantry to close with the enemy and to drive deep into his position in order to crush all resistance or to annihilate him. This end can be accomplished only if the hostile automatic weapons and artillery are neutralized or destroyed. Coordination between infantry and artillery must at all times and in all situations be carefully arranged.

When tanks and infantry are operating together, they both should be initially assigned the same objective, namely, the hostile artillery. Tanks can often attack from a different direction. The coordination of other weapons of the division attacking with tanks is based on the activities of the latter. The division commander is responsible for such coordination. Artillery supports the tank attack by firing upon antitank weapons, blinding hostile observation, and neutralizing villages and edges of woods. Artillery fire must be carefully observed and controlled to preclude firing upon friendly tanks and advancing troops. Engineer troops remove tank obstacles and assist tank units forward. The air force provides connection between the fast-moving tank units, the division, and the artillery. Combat aviation may be employed to neutralize antitank weapons.

Antiaircraft troops protect the deployment of troops, positions of readiness, artillery positions, and battle reconnaissance planes. The main effort must receive the bulk of antiaircraft protection. Gas may be used against artillery and reserves, and in connection with road blocks or blockades on an open flank. The communications net will be based upon the plan of maneuver; separate nets for artillery and infantry will be established, the artillery net having priority.

50. ATTACKING A POSITION

The plan of attack will be determined by the situation, the morale of the enemy, and the extent of his defensive works. Approach to the hostile position may be possible only under cover of darkness. If the position cannot be turned or enveloped, then a penetration must be made through some point in the front. The employment of inadequate force and means leads to severe reverses.

Careful plans for the attack must include the necessary information about the enemy and the terrain.[22] Thorough reconnaissance must be conducted by the officers of all arms, but reconnaissance parties must be kept restricted in size. Air reconnaissance is of particular value. Observation and listening posts must be established. Limited- objective attacks, strong combat patrols, and similar methods may be necessary to gain the information desired.

The location of the main effort will be determined by friendly intentions, the situation, the defensive strength of the hostile position, the covered approaches, and the observation for supporting weapons, particularly the artillery. In selecting a place for a

---

[22] The following points should be clarified: Where are the enemy's advanced positions, outpost lines, main line of resistance, switch positions, reserves, and observation posts? Where does the terrain favor the approach and the attack? Where has the enemy employed gas and obstacles?

penetration or break-through, consider the following points:

(a) Find out how the attack can be further developed after the initial break-through, (b) Insure sufficient room for maneuver, (c) Avoid natural strongpoints or envelop them, (d) Locate favorable terrain for the employment of tanks, (e) Capture points or areas that will give good observation deep into hostile positions. (f) Designate close or far-distant objectives according to the size of the attacking unit: if the final objective cannot be reached in one advance, designate intermediate objectives involving in some cases limited-objective attacks.

51. ARTILLERY EMPLOYMENT

Under the protection of advance infantry units, the artillery will be brought forward. Prompt reconnaissance of the terrain must be carefully made by artillery officers in small groups. If possible, positions for the batteries should be so placed that the artillery mission may be carried out without change of locations. Ammunition supply, observation, hostile position, communications, alternate positions, and range must all be considered, and any necessary preparations carried out in advance. The distribution of the artillery will be determined by its mission, Units will usually be employed intact; it may, however, be necessary to detach batteries, particularly the heavy artillery. In very narrow division sectors, for example, heavy howitzer batteries may be taken away from divisions to operate against distant targets under corps.

The initial mission of the artillery may include any or all of the following: firing upon important targets in the battlefield, drawing the fire of hostile artillery, engaging in counterbattery work against hostile artillery and anti- aircraft batteries as early as possible, and firing upon large hostile group movements at maximum ranges and as promptly as possible.

52. INFANTRY POSITION OF READINESS (BEREITSTELLUNG)

The following considerations for an infantry "position of readiness" may be listed as follows:

(a) Avoid too close proximity to the enemy position in cases where no cover is available to friendly troops, (b) If the enemy has previously offered strong resistance in the fighting, if there is reason to avoid premature entrance into the effective hostile defensive area, or if the enemy situation in the main battle position is not clarified, have the troops partially developed before they are conducted forward in their respective zones of action, (c) Avoid hostile air and ground obstruction by prohibiting large assemblies in restricted areas, by exploiting all ground folds and available cover, and by approaching immediately prior to the jump-off as close to the hostile position as cover permits, (d) Select the infantry jump-off position as close as possible to the hostile position in order to permit the artillery to push well forward and carry out its mission without changing location.[23] (e) Establish local security with infantry detachments. (f) Gain sufficient depth by drawing out and retaining reserves to the rear, (g) If the forces going into the position of readiness are scheduled to make a close-in envelopment, insure that the position is a sufficient distance off to the side to preclude the enveloping force advancing into and mixing with other friendly troops on the flank, when the attack is launched.

53. INFANTRY ACTION UP TO THE FIRST ASSAULT

---

[23] When the terrain and available cover do not permit the close approach of the infantry, the artillery must be echeloned to the rear and prepared to support the infantry advance on the enemy position.

The infantry action up to the first assault is carried out under the support of artillery and heavy infantry weapons. If exceptionally strong artillery support is available, the infantry can more freely advance against the enemy position; if the artillery support is not strong, however, then the infantry must advance cautiously. In the latter case, moving forward under cover of darkness or of smoke, the infantry takes advantage of cover to avoid hostile observation and of defiladed ground to avoid hostile fire.

The infantry attack begins with the advance of the light weapons under cover of the fire of artillery and heavy infantry weapons. Part of the latter should be pushed forward with the initial echelons to insure continual close support. Riflemen work forward through the use of fire and movement. Local fire superiority must be exploited to the fullest degree to capture ground. Those units or parts of units which cannot advance farther should dig in and hold tenaciously the ground already won. When weak points in the hostile position are found, they should be attacked aggressively and with reserves. Thus a push forward can be made. Against consolidated and extensive defensive works on the other hand, the infantry may struggle for days, working slowly forward. Trenches and terrain may be won, lost, and rewon during the course of the action.

54. ARTILLERY SUPPORT OF THE INFANTRY ADVANCE

The effectiveness of counterbattery missions directed by the artillery commander depends upon observation and available ammunition. Neutralization was often accomplished in World War I by a simultaneous concentration of several batteries using gas shells. Initially many batteries may be concealed in a firing position awaiting the opportunity to surprise the enemy. When new hostile batteries are discovered or additional enemy forces[24] are located, then concentrated fire may be delivered upon them with these batteries. This method is much more economical in ammunition than continual fire of all artillery against apparent but not definitely identified targets.

As the situation develops and clarifies, artillery fire can be switched from the manifestly less important targets to the more important areas. The infantry will sometimes be unavoidably delayed in its advance by reason of changes in the infantry-artillery plan of coordination. There will be situations in which many

---

[24] Artillery engages the hostile infantry which is fighting on the flank or in front of friendly infantry.

hostile batteries will not be located until friendly infantry has pushed forward and drawn fire.

55. INTERMITTENT ADVANCE OF THE RESERVES

At the disposal of the commander, the reserves follow beyond range of hostile fire. When the terrain permits, their advance should be made by bounds from cover to cover.

56. BREAK-THROUGH

a. *Penetration of the Hostile Position*

The timing of the assault is determined either by the forward echelons or by the commander himself. No hard and fast rule can be applied. Should the foremost units recognize the opportunity to push through, they must take full and quick advantage, calling upon supporting weapons for intensified fire to support their assault. When the infantry is observed advancing rapidly on the hostile position, this increased support may under certain circumstances occur automatically. Should the commander order the assault — avoiding an elaborate plan — he must quickly concentrate his strength at the point of penetration.

b. *Time of Attack*

Daybreak is often considered the most favorable time to gain surprise for the attack. War experience indicates, however, that daybreak is the time of highest alertness, and it is better to change continually the hour of attack. The time of attack should usually be postponed if the artillery has not completed all of its preparations. An attack against a position must be supported by artillery which is fully prepared to carry out its missions. In order to penetrate a stubbornly defended main line of resistance, concentrations of fire by all weapons must be arranged.

c. *Enemy Withdrawals*

If the enemy withdraws to rearward positions (a move generally accomplished at night), the following action should be taken: (a) Maintain close contact with the hostile infantry, (b) Promptly reconnoiter the new hostile positions, (c) Move the artillery well forward, (d) Prepare for hostile counterattacks, (e) On the following day, push rapidly forward with all force; compel the enemy to stand and fight, to take flight, or to suffer destruction.

57. ACTION RECOMMENDED FOR CERTAIN SPECIAL CASES

If the enemy has had only a short time in which to prepare his defensive position, if the morale of the enemy is shaken, or if the possibility of surprise is introduced, the preparations for attacking a position may be shortened to limited reconnaissance, more rapid development and preparation by the artillery, and employment of tanks and smoke screens.

If the enemy resorts to delaying action, the response should be to break through his line at one point and exploit the break with strong force, and to press closely upon the withdrawing hostile troops.

If the enemy falls behind the cover of a very strong position, the direction or location of the main effort should be changed. Knowledge of the terrain will permit advance planning in this maneuver. More artillery, tanks, and engineer troops should be moved well forward, and minimum requirements should be established in the communication system. If the enemy succeeds in falling back upon an entirely new and very strong defensive position, a regrouping of the attacking forces and new plans may be required.

If the attack continues until nightfall without producing decisive results, the regrouping of the command should be carried on under cover of darkness. The day's battle experience may indicate a new point for the main effort, and the order for attack should be issued just as early as possible. Reconnaissance must be energetic and continued, for the enemy will also make changes in his disposition during darkness. Night attacks are useful in determining hostile intentions and movements, in seizing favorable positions for the following day's jump-off, and in obtaining observation. Harassing fire by the artillery and air night-bombing attacks should be scheduled. Artillery support may not be possible at dawn of the following day, unless the exact enemy positions have been located. Only then can the artillery deliver unobserved supporting fires. Sufficient light for artillery observations should be awaited in preference to sending the infantry forward unsupported. Artillery on other fronts may be fired for deceptive purposes during the interval of waiting.

Passing over to the defense from the attack may be a necessary prelude to holding captured ground, or may be ordered by higher authority. Troops in either case are reorganized, and unnecessary forces withdrawn.

Artillery must protect the relief of friendly infantry by heavy concentrations and counter battery fire.

58. MEETING ENGAGEMENT

a. *Speed and Surprise*

In a meeting engagement, it is possible (though improbable with modern far-reaching reconnaissance and intelligence means) that the first information of the presence of the enemy will be received through actual contact. Initially the situation is vague and the security of both forces uncertain. A meeting engagement must not be permitted to develop into a wild rush upon the hostile position; a coordinated plan must be carried out calmly, but so accelerated as to carry out the following considerations: (a) Seize the initiative and fix the hostile force insofar as the situation permits, (b) Expedite preparations for the attack, quickly occupying ground favorable for observation, development, and advance, and for supporting weapons, (c) Intensify reconnaissance, ground and air, to determine promptly the enemy's dispositions, strength, intentions, and weaknesses, (d) Surprise the enemy, principally by rapidity of movement and by screening your troops and movements prior to entrance into battle.

b. *Time and Space*

The advance guard of each march column must provide time and space for development by the main body. An energetic advance under cover of the advance guard artillery often seizes important terrain features to the front and flanks, and fixes the hostile force. By extending over a broad front with its infantry and artillery, the advance guard can deceive the enemy relative to strength and movements.

c. *Coordination*

In a meeting engagement in open terrain and when the enemy has excellent observation, it is necessary to develop and prepare for combat much earlier than otherwise. The location of the main effort is promptly communicated to the various columns, and they deploy in keeping with the general plan in order to insure coordination of effort. The prompt employment of additional artillery support should be coordinated with the general scheme of maneuver,

d. *Methods*

In attacking during a meeting engagement, alternative methods exist for utilizing the main body: (a) prompt employment as the units of the march columns reach the immediate combat area; (b) development, and occupation of a position of readiness from which, the attack will be launched. In the first case, the units will be issued individual orders as they arrive.[25] All unit commanders must insure coordination between their infantry and supporting weapons. In the second case, the attack will be conducted similarly to an attack against an enemy in position. It will not be advantageous to push through an attack immediately if the terrain is difficult or if the employment of the mass of the force on the same day is no longer possible. The action of neighboring units must also be taken into consideration.

59. PURSUIT

The absolute disregard of all factors except the annihilation of the hostile force will govern the conduct of the pursuit. The most important principles involved are to harass continually the hostile force in front and on the flanks, and to block the avenues of retreat. It is

---

[25] The situation may so develop that the immediate employment of units as they arrive will not be necessary. The remainder will then be first moved into positions of readiness.

most important that the intention of the enemy to withdraw be promptly recognized.[26] When such recognition becomes definite, the commander will immediately employ all available force and spare no effort in order to annihilate the enemy. Premature pursuit can result disastrously; on the other hand, if the withdrawing enemy is permitted time in which to break off combat, an opportunity for decisive victory may be lost; the commander must therefore carefully consider the situation and evaluate the information prior to committing his troops to the pursuit. Commanders of subordinate units in the forward echelon push energetically forward when the enemy gives way. The presence of higher commanders in these forward units spurs the troops to greater effort.

Some of the important considerations for conducting successful pursuits are: (a) Employ air force units against large bodies of hostile retreating troops; use reconnaissance planes to determine direction of withdrawal and use diving attacks with machine guns and bombs upon troops and materiel in marching columns, especially in defiles and against bridges, (b) Employ artillery in harassing missions. Let part of the

---

[26] Clues may be derived from airplane reports of rearward movements of trains, supply, echelons, and reserves; from reports from friendly troops; and from patrolling, particularly at night, and miscellaneous signal interceptions.

long-range artillery pound vigorously on potential avenues of withdrawal, roads, etc., and keep the bulk of the artillery leap-frogging rapidly, pressing close behind the friendly infantry to render support, (c) Employ infantry in pushing rapidly forward literally on the heels of the withdrawing enemy; assign distant objectives in the direction of the withdrawal; have the heavy infantry weapons follow closely the forward echelon; and give the enemy no time to organize a defense, (d) Employ engineers to repair roads in the rear of the pursuing forces, to remove obstacles, and to neutralize gassed areas.

While the frontal attack is vigorously carried out, enveloping forces of great mobility[27] will operate from flank and rear against the hostile retreating columns. Defiles, bridges, and favorable observation deep in rear of the enemy will be seized, and avenues of retreat cut off. If the enemy succeeds in organizing a delaying position, a coordinated attack must be promptly arranged and launched.

Commanders must insure a continual flow of supplies for the rapidly advancing units. In pursuit, matters of supply and evacuation require particularly careful supervision.

---

[27] Motorized infantry, mounted troops, motorized engineers, and antitank and antiaircraft units.

Pursuing troops must maintain contact with the enemy, and must report back frequently to headquarters their own locations. If the pursuit continues into the night, infantry units push forward along the roads. Artillery continues long-range harassing fire, while individual batteries follow the infantry in close proximity for rendering immediate support.[28]

---

[28] Artillery firing at night under such conditions is, of course, map firing.

A German column under attack by the Fenrik Kvaals resistance group in Norway.

Section XIII. THE DEFENSE

The important considerations of defense are combined in utilization of terrain and coordination of fire. The natural defensive characteristics of the terrain should be improved, and camouflage should be used freely. A fully coordinated use of all available weapons must be arranged; strength should be conserved by keeping the losses in personnel and materiel down to the very minimum; and exact dispositions, strength, and intentions should be denied to the enemy as long as possible. A well-organized defense capable of quickly and effectively reverting to the attack, with cunning and deception enshrouding the movements and dispositions, will offset hostile numerical superiority.

60. FAVORABLE TERRAIN FOR DEFENSE

The defender has an advantage in that he selects the terrain for his battle. Rarely will all of the following terrain requirements for defense exist in a single combat area, but certain of them will be present, and the commander may improvise the others: (a) good observation for artillery and other supporting weapons; (b) protection against hostile observation; (c) natural obstacles against tank attacks; (d) natural protection for flanks; (e) possibility for launching counterattacks.

61. OTHER CONSIDERATIONS

a. *Defense or Delaying Action?*

The mission must clearly indicate the form, of defense contemplated: defense (Verteidigung), meaning that the position will be held under all circumstances; or delaying action (Hinhaltender Widerstand). Fire may be opened either at maximum effective ranges, if the ammunition is ample, or at closer ranges, in order to effect surprise.

b. *Preparation of Defense Area*

When the hostile situation has not been clarified (especially if the direction of the enemy's attack is unknown), the mass of the defending force should be retained in a position of readiness. When information relative to hostile formations, main effort, strength, etc., becomes, available, then the troops may be moved into defensive positions which have been previously reconnoitered and prepared according to the time available and the situation. Occasionally only a skeleton position will be occupied with artillery protected by small units of infantry, while the mass is held back centrally located so that it can quickly occupy positions upon the approach of the enemy.

c. *Maneuvers*

Advanced positions and outposts delay him and give time for the occupation and preparation of favorable defense terrain. Reserves are used for flank protection, for counterattacks, and for blocking penetrations. Fire power must never be weakened by holding out unnecessarily large reserves. If, after contact with the enemy, the situation requires defensive maneuver, the position is quickly organized as the troops deploy, and if the terrain is not particularly favorable, the troops are drawn back to better defensive terrain.

62. GENERAL PRINCIPLES OF DEFENSE

Some of the general principles of defense can be summarized as follows: (a) The purpose of the defense is to nullify the hostile attack, (b) The position selected is held to the last; the commander may under certain circumstances, however, restrict the time, (c) The defensive position selected must compel the enemy either to attack, relinquish the advance, or attempt to avoid combat.[29] (d) Hostile envelopments are countered by extending or refusing the flank (or flanks), or by echelonment of reserves, (e) If the enemy attempts to march around in order to avoid the position entirely, then he should be attacked.

63. ORGANIZATION OF DEFENSE AREAS

a. Defense in Depth

---

[29] This can be accomplished if the position cannot be entirely a, voided or enveloped by the enemy.

The main battle position is organized in depth to accomplish dense all-around fires and effectively limit hostile penetrations. Local withdrawals before superior hostile fire may be authorized by the regimental commander to his battalion commanders, or, in special cases, by the latter to their subordinates; local withdrawals must not, however, permit the loss of connection between units in the line or hostile penetration into the main battle zone. In terrain not too unfavorable for the defense, units occupy fronts double the width of those assigned for the attack. These islands of resistance are so organized as to permit all-around defense, with weapons so sighted as to cover all possible avenues of approach at maximum ranges.

The defensive zone is organized in depth, with the main line of resistance in front of the terrain that is favorable for observation posts for the artillery and heavy supporting weapons. The higher commander selects the general defensive line on the map and assigns sectors to units. Subordinate commanders carefully reconnoiter the terrain and select the locations for their troops and various types of weapons.

b. *Cover and Obstacles*

Cover for machine-gun emplacements; observation posts, and accompanying weapons is provided. Obstacles are constructed to supplement the natural defensive characteristics of the terrain. Priorities of defensive works are governed by the rule that "effectiveness of fire takes priority over cover." The normal order of tasks is the following:[30] (a) clearing fields of fire and establishing distances to increase the efficiency of fire; (b) camouflaging installations and erecting dummy establishments; (c) constructing splinter cover for observation posts; (d) constructing machine-gun emplacements; (e) erecting barbed wire or other obstacles; (f) excavating dug-outs, switch positions, or planned communication routes.

64. RESERVES, RELIEFS, AND REAR POSITIONS

Local reserves are used to fill in gaps in the line, to counterattack against a local penetration, and to relieve troops in the front line. General reserves are used to protect a flank, to counterattack against a serious penetration, to counterattack when the situation

---

[30] Several of these tasks, such as camouflaging, may be undertaken concurrently with other tasks.

indicates a return to offensive tactics, and to relieve organizations in the line.

A relief is only effected after a long period of defense, and under cover of darkness. Infantry and artillery are never relieved simultaneously. The relief order directs when and where the relief is to report, the routes to be used by the relieving force and the troops relieved; and the time when the new commander is definitely to assume responsibility for the sector.

Only necessary under exceptional circumstances, rear positions must be located sufficiently back from the main line of resistance to require the enemy artillery to move forward. A rear position will be ordered occupied by the commander when the former position can be held only with unjustifiable losses and when consideration for adjacent units does not forbid.

65. ACTUAL OPERATION OF THE DEFENSE

a. *Main Line of Resistance*

All fires along the main line of resistance and in the principal defensive zone are carefully coordinated to insure that all areas, particularly the potential avenues of approach, are covered by strong concentrations. Artillery and infantry are coordinated to permit a rapid switch from one area to another; and fire plans are prepared to limit penetrations and to block envelopments.

Defensive preparations are secured from hostile observation by active reconnaissance and by a screening force, both of which operate under the same commander.

Generous use of obstacles, natural and constructed, is made. The advanced troops are under direct control of the commander; after fighting in delaying action before superior enemy forces, they withdraw to rearward positions as prearranged by him.

b. *Advance Position*

The advance position, usually located within the sphere of operation of friendly long-range artillery in the main battle position, is occupied to prevent the early seizure of important terrain features by the enemy. Camouflage and dummy works are used freely. The advance position increases the effectiveness and the time of employment of long-range artillery by protecting advanced, artillery observation posts; also, such a position deceives the enemy relative to the dispositions and organization for defense, and causes him to deploy prematurely. Friendly troops must withdraw before the enemy can overrun the position. In withdrawing, prearranged routes will be indicated to insure that the fire of weapons located in the next position to the rear (outpost line of resistance) is not masked.

c. *Outpost Position*

The outpost position, located within the sphere of operation of the light artillery batteries in the main position, is selected to provide time for troops manning the main defensive position to prepare for action, to supplement observation, and to deceive the attacker relative to dispositions. Troops from infantry units immediately to the rear generally occupy this line and are withdrawn by signal according to prearranged plan so that fields before the main line of resistance are not obstructed. Artillery delays the hostile approach by the use of harassing fires controlled by radio reports from advanced observation posts. To increase radius of action, a few light batteries may be advanced forward to locations between the outpost line and the advance position.

66. ARTILLERY IN THE DEFENSE

a. *Control by Artillery Commander*

The commander of the whole defensive force determines the proportion of artillery to be held in direct support and the proportion to be attached to infantry units. Artillery is kept as far as possible under the control of the artillery commander, who under all circumstances retains control of the mass of the division artillery. If the situation permits and there is an ample ammunition supply, heavy fires may be delivered at long ranges.

b. *Tactics*

In the initial stages of a defensive action, artillery may sometimes be kept silent to facilitate deception; otherwise, it will be employed to draw hostile artillery fire, to deliver counterbattery fires, or to bring down harassing fires on the approaching hostile infantry. In the advanced stages of a defensive action, the bulk of the artillery is used to deliver concentrations on hostile positions of readiness, and particularly on hostile heavy infantry weapons; the remainder is used to deliver counterbattery fire. And in the final stage — when the hostile force is on the point of launching its assault — the artillery delivers preparations and barrages upon the hostile assault.

c. *Barrage*

Should the enemy make a surprise attack at night or in a fog, a barrage of all weapons is delivered immediately in front of the main line of resistance. Definite restrictions relative to coverage and duration of fire are issued.[31] As a rule, heavy artillery does not participate.

67. INFANTRY IN THE DEFENSE

With part of their heavy weapons, the infantry opens fire upon the approaching enemy at good distance; if friendly artillery support is weak, at maximum ranges. Firing positions are located in advance of the main line of resistance or in the forward part of the defensive area. As the enemy draws closer, he is engaged by the fire of all the defending heavy weapons, and finally by the fire of all available weapons. The infantry fills up gaps in the line, recapturing any sections temporarily lost.

68. HOSTILE PENETRATIONS

---

[31] In this connection a light howitzer battery (105-mm) can cover about 160 meters (175 yards); a light battalion, about 500 meters (550 yards).

Where small groups of the enemy have broken through, the groups should be destroyed immediately. Box barrages placed in their rear will preclude their withdrawal. When a successful break-through of large pro- portions has been accomplished by the enemy, the commander of the defensive force will decide whether the position will be shifted or the lost ground regained by counterattack. If he decides to counterattack, the fires of all weapons are carefully coordinated, a limited objective is assigned, and air and tank support is provided.

69. THE COUNTERATTACK

It is most important that the psychological moment be recognized for the counterblow. The commander is ever alert for indications.[32] The counterattack plan resembles a limited-objective attack in which artillery support, boundaries, and objectives are specified. Any objective selected must be a decisive terrain feature.

70. WITHDRAWAL TO A REARWARD POSITION

---

[32] Hostile repulses, heavy losses, enemy errors, morale of the enemy, or morale of friendly troops.

Advance orders are issued to effect a withdrawal, thus ensuring coordination. Contact with adjacent units is maintained. The movement to the rear is effected under cover of darkness.[33] Activity on the original position will be simulated to deceive the enemy. Firing by part of the infantry and artillery will be continued from the forward position to give the enemy the impression that it is still being strongly defended. The hostile advance upon the new (renewed) position will be delayed by the fire of artillery and heavy weapons, supplemented by means of poison gas and obstacles.

---

[33] Daylight withdrawals are only attempted under cover of fog, artificial or natural, or over terrain of very restricted visibility, when the situation definitely indicates that it will be dangerous to wait until darkness.

German troops in Russia, 1943.

Section XIV. THE DELAYING ACTION

The purpose of a delaying action is to effect maximum delay to the enemy without committing the friendly force to decisive action. It is employed to avoid breaking before superior hostile force; to gain time or to improve the situation with reference to observation, cover, and field of fire; and to maneuver the enemy into a position in which he may be more effectively attacked. If a transition from defense to delaying action is imperative, the first position selected should be at least 6 miles to the rear. A fully coordinated attack by the enemy can be checked by causing him to displace his artillery and to reorganize generally before he launches a new attack.

The characteristic organization for delaying action includes the following considerations: (a) Successive defensive lines are selected with sufficient intervals to cause displacement of the enemy's artillery. (b) Positions selected should permit distant observation and effective use of long-range weapons, and have cover in the rear to facilitate withdrawal, (c) Natural obstacles are fully exploited and supplemented by constructed obstacles and by the use of poison gas. (d) The bulk of the artillery, along with the long-range artillery, is held under the artillery commander for long-range interdiction and counterbattery missions, (e) Resistance in the forward position is continued until the next rearward position is occupied and fully prepared to carry on the defense. (f) Units are deployed over very broad fronts and with no depth.[34] (g) Small reserves are retained, (h) Reserves are utilized to cover the withdrawal particularly by daylight (according to the situation and terrain, they may be located off to a flank or on a commanding piece or terrain, which facilities the protection of the units withdrawing), (i) When the situation permits, withdrawals are always made under

---

[34] In favorable terrain a unit may occupy a sector twice as wide as is normal for defense. In heavily wooded areas or where visibility is restricted, the sectors are narrower.

cover of darkness; sometimes, even at the risk of being involved in serious action requiring a strong defense, the situation should be held until darkness.

German troops falling back with a wounded comrade.

Section XV. RETREAT-RETIREMENT

In a retreat-retirement, contact with the enemy is broken off for the purpose of seeking more favorable terrain or conditions for the resumption of offensive action. A commander may be forced by the trend of circumstances to retire, or he may, of his own free will, elect to retire. Only the greatest emergency is considered to justify retreat. Local reverses should not be taken seriously. No second-in-command upon receipt of un- favorable information is authorized to order a retreat. If the situation indicates the necessity, he must report to a higher commander and state his intentions to retire with the reasons therefore.

A retreat should be effected under cover of darkness, with the greatest secrecy. If troops are told the purpose — to improve their future chance of success — their morale will not be adversely affected. Fresh troops if available should be given the mission of rear and flank guards to protect the assembly and movement of the command. If the enemy is employing motorized or mechanized troops, special provision will have to be made to protect the flanks with antitank weapons and road blocks.

German artillery in North Africa, 1943.

Section XVI. THE EMPLOYMENT OF FIELD ARTILLERY

The division artillery commander is a special advisor to the division commander on artillery employment, replacement, and ammunition; he is also commander of the artillery regiment, which includes the medium howitzer battalion, the sound-and-flash battalion, and such artillery as may be attached. He orders artillery concentrations, counterbattery, and harrassing fire in cooperation with the general scheme of maneuver and in support of the infantry.

The artillery battalion is the fire unit. The battalion commander indicates definitely to his batteries such matters as the following: targets, aiming points, amounts of ammunition to be fired, time for opening fire, location of positions, ammunition supply, routes, type's of fire, and kinds of ammunition. Firing data are obtained for the battalion by ranging shots, map computations, operations of the observation battalion (sound-and-flash), and references furnished by friendly troops. In very wide sectors or when operating in terrain of restricted visibility, it may be necessary for certain batteries to obtain firing data individually according to their tactical missions.

71. ORGANIZATION

Part of the artillery, usually the light howitzers, has the principal mission of providing direct support to the infantry. The remainder is employed in counterbattery, harassing fires and preparations, concentrations, and interdictions. Close connection with the sound-and-flash battalion is maintained. Disposition must be kept flexible to permit quick shifting of battery positions, missions, and targets. The employment in general is determined by these considerations: (a) number and kinds of guns available; (b) combat plans of the command as a whole; (c) terrain and weather; (d) hostile artillery; (e) ammunition available.

72. LOCATION IN THE ATTACK

In general, in the attack the artillery is located immediately in rear of the infantry line, just beyond range of hostile small-arms fire. Figure 1 shows a typical arrangement, with the observation battalion (sound-and-flash) operating directly under the artillery commander.

If reconnaissance and combat intelligence have given definite information about hostile dispositions, then a preparation may be fired, continuing 10 to 30 minutes, and depending upon the ammunition available, the surprise effect, and the situation. In the case where practically no information on the enemy is available, the artillery preparation is omitted; the infantry launches the attack, drawing fire from hostile heavy weapons and artillery, upon which, once located, the friendly artillery can thereafter fire.

73. LOCATION IN THE DEFENSE

Artillery in the defense is organized the same way as in the attack. The only difference in dispositions is that the direct support weapons (light howitzers) are located slightly farther to the rear, and the general support guns (medium howitzers) are in a central location where they can interdict at long ranges to force an early deployment of approaching enemy formations.

74. COOPERATION WITH INFANTRY

Time and space must be carefully coordinated by both the infantry and the artillery. It is essential that the artillery observers be at all times alert, not only to locate targets and hostile forces but to follow closely the movements of friendly troops, particularly the infantry. To facilitate this close contact, it devolves upon the infantry to seize and hold terrain which offers excellent observation for the artillery, Communication is effectively maintained. Close contact between infantry and artillery officers is absolutely essential. The division commander indicates, as promptly as possible, the plan of maneuver to the artillery commander so as to permit the latter the maximum freedom in planning the role for the artillery.

In the advance the artillery renders immediate support to the infantry when contact with the enemy is gained. This is accomplished by the artillery observers, who accompany the foremost infantry elements, or observe from balloon or airplane. In the attack the artillery must neutralize the hostile resistance and open the way for the advance of the infantry. Rapid reconnaissance and prompt deployment for action contribute to the success of this mission. It is generally advantageous for the infantry to wait for the support of the artillery. It is also important for the infantry to understand the limitations and capabilities of the artillery.[35]

---

[35] In this connection: (1) the number, caliber, and effective range of batteries available; (2) the time necessary for preparation of fire; (3) the amount and kind of ammunition available; (4) the type of targets adapted to artillery fire.

Nr. 939783

Bescheinigung

über Inanspruchnahme durch die Deutsche Wehrmacht Mottatt

‒ DES 1943

An

1.   Kommune Trondheim
      (Name und Anschrift des in Anspruch genommenen Norwegers)

2. den Bürgermeister (Ordfører)   D r o n t h e i m

     den Lensmann in   ./.

3. das Innenriksdepartement — Oppgjörsavdelingen — O s l o , Grubbegaten 9

Die Deutsche Wehrmacht nimmt mit Wirkung vom   6. 11. 1943

das Grundstück
           (genaue Bezeichnung nach Gegenstand und Lage)

im Grundstück Trondheim kommunale   folgende Räume   Mellemilen
      Middelskole   (Lage)   (Turnhalle)
                                         130 qm

in Anspruch. Eigentümer bzw. Besitzer ist   Kommune Trondheim.

           (genaue Bezeichnung mit Namen und Vornamen, Firma usw.)

Die Inanspruchnahme erstreckt sich auf die im Grundstück befindlichen Einrichtungsgegenstände,

insbesondere   ./.

           (möglichst genaue Aufführung der übernommenen Gegenstände)

Mit übernommen sind Feuerungsmaterialvorräte im Werte von   ./.   Kronen.

Die Entschädigung wird nicht durch die Wehrmacht, sondern durch den Bürgermeister *)

in   D r o n t h e i m   Lensmann *) in   ./.   gezahlt.

*) Nichtzutreffendes durchstreichen.

Anfragen können an die Stadtkommandantur
-Abt.Unterkunft- in D r o n t h e i m
oder an die Dienststelle der Feldpost-
Nr. 26099 G gerichtet werden.

Vermerk für die norwegischen Abrechnungsbehörden:

Die Wehrmacht hat dem in Anspruch genommenen Norweger bisher Vergütung in Höhe

von monatlich   ./.   Kronen gezahlt und Ein- bzw. Umbauten im Werte von

etwa   ./.   Kronen vorgenommen.

Druck: AOK Norwegen

*Captured German document regarding the Wehrmacht
and a citizen of Norway.*

APPENDIX. SAMPLE GERMAN ORDERS

Examples of four different German orders are given below in English translation.[36] Though slightly awkward in expression, the literal rendering tends to give the reader a more accurate conception, both as to contents and as to structure. The English text is, however, much longer than the original German, partly because several English words are sometimes needed to carry the thought expressed in a single German word and partly because most of the German military abbreviations have been translated in full.

1. Example A.

I Army Corps

 GUT EIMERSHAUSEN

Operations Section No. –

 12.4, 1915[37]

Warning Order

1. Our rear guards withdrew before weak enemy attacks. A long hostile column was observed marching

---

[36] Examples of German combat orders in the German language are included in "The German Rifle Company, For Study and Translation," Information Bulletin, No. 15, May 16, 1942, pp. 295-307.

[37] This is the date and hour of the order, namely April 12, at 1915 (7.15 p. m.). Dates and time are similarly indicated throughout this and the other orders presented here.

east on the road: BUREN — WINNENBERG — FÜRSTENBERG (head of column here by 1700).

2. I Army Corps continues to retire on CASSEL on 13.4, marching to position behind the FULDA RIVER, where it will establish a defensive position.

3. The 2d and 3d Inf Divs will march upon CASSEL at 0400, with the heads of their main bodies crossing the line: VOLKMARSEN — WOLFHAGEN — IPPINGHAUSEN and the northernmost column of the 2d Inf. Div. over EHRINGEN — OBERELSUNGEN — DÜRNBERG.

The rear guards evacuate their present positions at 0300 and withdraw to the line: VOLKMARSEN — WOLFHAGEN — NAUMBERG. This line will be held at least until 13.4, 1400.

4. The 1st Inf Div withdraws upon HANN MUNDEN. It will cover the wing and flank of the I Corps Boundary between 1st and 2d Divs: BILLENGSHAUSEN — RHODEN — BREUNA — EHRSTEN — SPEELE — WEDEMUNDEN (all to 1st Div).

5. Corps Commander goes at 0300 to DÜRNBERG, in the course of the morning to ESCHERODA. Reports to DÜRNBERG after 0500.

Sent by Officer

in passenger car.

X

Lt General

2. EXAMPLE B

COMPLETE COMBAT ORDER (CORPS)

III Army Corps	Corps
Headquarters	
General Staff Section—	PRIEDRICHRODA
Operations No. 3	21.4., 1900

Corps Order for the Attack on 24.4

1. In the hostile positions along the Corps front there have been no essential changes noted and enemy will continue to defend his position. Improvement of fieldworks continues. Aerial photographs of the front taken on the morning 20.4. will be distributed today to all units down to include battalions. In the sector GR VARGULA — ALTGURNA along the UMSTRUTT

RIVER, work on a rearward defensive position has been noted.

2. The I Army Corps attacks at X hour on 24.4. in its present combat zone and destroys the hostile force south of the UMSTRUTT. Strong forces will follow the Corps in the 2d line available to exploit a break-through.

Attack Objective of the Corps on 24.4:

High ground northeast and north of ASCHARA — WIE-GLEBEN — STEIN B — north edge GR HARTH.

3. Reconnaissance. — a. Reconnaissance Echelon (H) 3 (Air) reconnoiter the Corps Combat Zone to include the UMSTRUTT RIVER during 22.4 and 23.4. Observe particularly for special hostile arrangements of dispositions. On 23.4 especially reconnoiter to locate hostile reserves, tank barriers, tank defense weapons, and tank units.

From daybreak 24.4 on are attached to:

    7th Division -- 1 Airplane

    8th Division -- 3 Airplanes

Planes available and prepared to fly missions beginning 24.4., 0430, from landing field FRIEDRICHRODA. Drop and pick-up field maintained until 24.4., 0430, as follows:

    by 7 Div at ALS B

by 8 Div southwest HAIN B

b. Battle reconnaissance by the divisions: through continual surveillance of the battlefield day and night, from 22.4 until 24.4, establish the location of changes involving hostile observation posts, antitank defense, MLR, artillery positions, road blocks and barriers, reserves. For reasons of deception the activity of patrols will not be increased.

4. Organization and Combat Zones for the Attack:

Right: 9th Div

Middle: 7th Div

Attached:

Corps Arty Btry 39

Hv Arty Btry 35 (only until 24.4, X + 2 hours)

Left: 8th Div

Attached:

Tk Brig 12

Army Arty Regt 101

Smoke Bn 102

Boundaries:

between 9th and 7th Divs: east edge ROCH-HEIM — west edge ASCHARA — east edge ECKARTSLEBEN — east edge ILLEBEN— 275.

between 7th and 8th Divs: east edge BRUHEIM — west edge GRUMBACH (STEIN B to 7th Div)— west edge UFHOVEN — west edge THAMSBRÜCK.

between 8th Div and I Army Corps: east edge

GROSSENBEHRINGEN — west slope 367— west part of GR. HARTH — west edge ALTERSTEDT— east edge GROSSENGOTTERN.

5. Conduct of Attack. —

a. *General.*

After an artillery preparation of 45 minutes, which will cover the approach of the infantry to the line: NESSE — BIEBER the infantry along the entire Corps front will attack, crossing over the NESSE-BIEBER line at X hour. Simultaneously in the 8th Div combat zone the landing waves of the Tank Brigade will cross the same line.

As 1st Attack Objective, the Corps and the neighboring divisions of the I and II Corps, will win the line: 334 (northeast from MOLSCHLEBEN) — ESCHENBERGEN — 292 (north from HAUSEN) — 309 (northeast from WESTHAUSEN)— north edge of WANGENHEIM — 278 (west from WANGENHEIM)— LOH B — TUNGE-DAER HEIGHTS — LEICH B — edge of wood north-west GROSSEN-BEHRINGEN — WARTEN B.

The Tank Brigade will drive its attack through to include the hostile artillery positions in the area: TUNGEDA — REICHENBACH — OSTERBEHRUNGEN — LOH B. Continuation of the attack after reaching 1st Objective only upon order of the Corps.

b. *Coordination of Time.*

X— 45 until X — 40 minutes: Surprise fire by all artillery to disturb hostile communications, reserves, and headquarters. Infantry and Tank Brigade begin to move into attack positions.

X — 40 until X —20 minutes: Counter battery fire by all artillery.

X-20 until X hour; Artillery fire upon hostile forward defensive positions. Smoking of B-STELLEN.[38] The 3d Div will smoke particularly the forest edge north of GROSSBEHRINGEN. X hour

Infantry and initial waves of Tank Brigade cross the line: NESSE-BIEBER B. Transfer of artillery fire to the hostile artillery positions rearward corresponding to the advance of the infantry attack. Simultaneously a box barrage around the point, of penetration fired by the artillery of the I and II Corps.

Early advance of positions of the mass of the light artillery to Hill 309 (9th Div)— 278 (7th Div) — LOH

---

[38] Observation posts.

B— THUNGEDAER — LORCH B (8th Div) will be arranged and carried out.

The Tank Brigade will, after reaching the 1st Objective and capturing the hostile artillery south of GR HARTB, assemble in the area BRUHEIM-FRIEDRICHWERTH awaiting further orders of the Corps Commander.

6. The Corps Artillery beginning with the artillery preparation will maintain fire, by the 150-mm artillery, upon the road: GRAFENTONNA — LANGESALZA — GROSSENGOTTERN.

7. Corps Antiaircraft Artillery — Part of Army AA. Art, Regt 104 and Army Pursuit Squadron: protect the preparation for the attack — defend the assembly areas from hostile
air observation and air attack. Special protection of the tank assembly ordered in paragraph 5b will be provided.

8. Corps Reserves.

29th Inf

Corps AT Bn

Corps Engr Bn

The 29th Inf will reconnoiter for covered approaches to and possible assembly areas in the area: FROTTSTEDT.

9. The Divisions will utilize to the fullest extent cover and camouflage in preparation for the attack.

Divisions will submit their attack and fire plans to the Corps Commander not later than 23.4, 1200. X hour will be announced at 23.4, 2300.

10. The Corps Command Post will remain at FRIEDRICHRODA until 24.4 (X— 30 when it will be established at HAIN B).

Distribution
    General of Infantry
"A"   B

3. EXAMPLE C SEPARATE ORDER (ARMY)

Army Commander
    Army Hq
General Staff Section I
    ALTENBURG, 1.12., 1500
Number —

To Res Inf Regt 19

1. Res Inf Regt 19 (with 1st Bn Res Arty Regt 7, 1st Co Res Engr Bn 7 attached) is attached to the X Army

Corps (Hq at WITTCHENDORF). It is expected that Res Inf Regt 19 will be employed on the west flank of the X Army Corps in the vicinity of SCHLEITZ.

2. Reinfd Res Inf Regt 19 will be transported in trucks (Trk Bn II) via SCHKÖLEN — EISENBERG — HERMSDORF to AUMA. March to begin from HAUMBTJRG not later than 2.12., 0000.

The Commander of the Truck Battalion II will report at 1630 in NAUMBURG to the Commander of the Res Inf Regt 19. The loading of troops into trucks in the bivouac area is not possible before 2200.

After the troops are unloaded in the new area, the Trk Bn II will march immediately to ZETZ.

3. The Commander of Res Inf Regt 19 will report at the COURT HOUSE in AUMA at 1.12., 0200, where he will receive further orders through the Commander of the X Corps.

(by Radio) For the Commander-in-Chief

4. EXAMPLE D

SPECIAL INSTRUCTIONS (DIVISION ADMINISTRATIVE ORDER)

1st Division

Division Command Post

General Staff Section

FRIEDENSTADT   8.10.,1930

IB

Number —

Special Instructions for Supply

(to Division Order Number — General Staff Section la,
8.10., 1930)

1. *Ammunition* — The supply of ammunition for the rear guards will be provided from the balances now in hands of troops and from the additional amounts to be delivered not later than 2200 to each regiment as follows:

75,000 rifle cartridges

1,000 hand grenades

130 flares

60 signal light cartridges

680 light infantry mortar shells

330 37-mm shells

The supply of ammunition for the artillery will be handled by the existing supply installations. Supply of ammunition for the Division Reconnaissance Battalion will be handled by 1st Infantry Regiment.

As reserve for the rear guards, ammunition will be left back in the present ammunition distributing point under guard, as follows:

100,000 armor-piercing cartridges

200 light infantry mortar shells

300 37-nim shells

600 105-mm light howitzer shells

The commander of the rear guard is responsible for the proper distribution of this reserve ammunition.

Place and time for issue of ammunition to the troops marching to the rear will be indicated later.

2. *Rations* — Rations and reduced iron rations for the rear guards will be left behind under guard as follows:

For rear guards in east sector: INGERSLEBEN CHURCH.

For remaining rear guards: GROSSRETTBACH CHURCH.

These rations will be collected by the rear-guard troops on 9.10., 0400.

Rations for remaining troops for 9.10. will be delivered to the bivouacs of March Groups A, B, and C, by means of supply column (animal-drawn) before 9.10., 0600. These supply columns will then remain with the march groups.

3. *Medical Service (Men).*

Collecting point (severely wounded) at FRIEDENSTADT.

Collecting point (lightly wounded) at GAMSTADT.

These collecting stations will be closed at 2100. The Med Co and Mtr Amb Plat (less section remaining with rear guard) will march to GRAFENRODA via KLEIMRETTBACH — BITTSTADT — GRAWINKEL.

Collecting point for wounded will be established in GOSSEL to open not later than 9.10., 0700.

The F Hosp will remain in ARNSTADT until 9.10., 0400, and will then be marched to SUHL. Wounded will be transported from ARNSTADT up to including 9.10., 0400, in hospital trains.

To take care of unforeseen losses (materiel) and wounded within the rear guards, one-half plat of the Med Co and 5 Mtr Arabs will remain in FRIEDENSTADT available to the Comdr of the rear guard.

4. *Medical Service (Animals).*